D1477156

Osprey AutoHistory

JAGUAR XJ
6 & 12, Daimler, Vanden Plas, XJ-S

Osprey AutoHistory

JAGUAR XJ
6 & 12, Daimler, Vanden Plas, XJ-S

CHRIS HARVEY

Published in 1980 by Osprey Publishing Limited,
12–14 Long Acre, London WC2E 9LP
Member company of the George Philip Group

United States distribution by

Osceola, Wisconsin 54020, USA

© Copyright Osprey Publishing Limited 1980

This book is copyrighted under the Berne Convention.
All rights reserved. Apart from any fair dealing for the
purpose of private study, research, criticism or review,
as permitted under the Copyright Act, 1956, no part of
this publication may be reproduced, stored in a retrieval
system, or transmitted in any form or by any means,
electronic, electrical, chemical, mechanical, optical,
photocopying, recording, or otherwise, without prior
written permission. All enquiries should be addressed to
the Publishers

British Library Cataloguing in Publication Data
Harvey, Chris
Jaguar XJ. – (Auto history; vol. 5)
1. Jaguar automobile
I. Title   II. Series
629.22′22   TL215.J3
ISBN 0-85045-364-X

Associate Michael Sedgwick

Design Giolitto, Wrigley and Couch

Filmset and printed in England
by BAS Printers Limited,
Over Wallop, Hampshire

Contents

Chapter 1
Such a Good Car?

Without a doubt, the Jaguar XJ saloons and everything that has sprung from them are the best cars the Coventry firm has ever made. The twelve-cylinder model has even been voted The Best Car in the World. Now the more mundane six-cylinder can vie for that title as fuel consumption plays a more important part in assessing any car. But no matter how many cylinders it has, the XJ has outsold all the Jaguars that went before, and some of them were mighty good cars. Jaguar XJ

The factory that gave birth to every Jaguar XJ, whether it be six-cylinder, twelve-cylinder, S type or their Daimler equivalents: Brown's Lane, Allesley, Coventry, pictured from the air

The man who made it all possible: Sir William Lyons, founder and President of Jaguar Cars, a brilliant stylist as well as businessman

production has been averaging 25,000 a year since 1969 with nearly a quarter of a million made at the time of writing. The earlier medium-sized saloons, mostly the Mark I and Mark II, but including the 420, from which the XJ was derived, sold the best part of 175,000 between 1955 and 1969. The larger Mark VII, VIII and IX saloons that were such outstanding designs in the 1950s sold only 47,000. The glorious sports cars, the XKs and E types, sold only 30,000 and 72,000 respectively. Only the medium-sized saloons had a longer production run and that is likely to be surpassed as the XJ continues to be produced in series III and XJ-S forms.

What makes the XJ such a good car? To understand that you have to go back to the beginning. The design was evidence of every lesson the great stylist Sir William Lyons benefited from in nearly fifty years at the helm of the firm that was to become Jaguar Cars. It was similarly the great work of his engineering team led by William Heynes, who had been with him since 1935. Other figures played their part, such as Wally Hassan and Bob Knight, the former the development engineer who brought with him years of experience and the latter a chassis engineer of no mean skill and now Managing as well as Technical Director of Jaguar Cars. But really the XJ belonged to Sir William and Heynes (Lyons called his trusted employees by their surnames in the good old 'British patriarchal tradition').

A lot of tradition went into the XJ, too. It followed established Jaguar practice of blending well-tried components from earlier models with brand-new design ideas. The new XJ, announced in September and introduced in October 1968, was a slimmer version of the bulbous 420G saloon produced in the 1960s; as lithe as any big cat!

With wider wheels and arches neatly incorporated into the car, the design emphasized the improvement in roadholding and ride without making the wheels, and car, look incongruous. The specially designed tyres did their job well, and managed to look efficient, even when the car was standing still. Additional glass in the new XJ distinguished it from its predecessors, emphasizing that Jaguars were keeping up with the

William Heynes, the brilliant engineer whose skill and dedication helped give the Jaguar XJ the title of the Best Car in the World

9

Geoffrey Robinson, the go-getter who took Jaguar Cars through a difficult period as Managing Director between 1973 and 1975 when other car manufacturers were floundering in the fuel crisis

changing times. But it revealed a traditionally luxurious interior, which proved that there was no accompanying decline in standards. The engine, the wonderful twin overhead cam XK which had taken the world by storm in 1948, was now at the peak of its development. The suspension was based on the highly successful all-independent system used on the E types and Jaguar saloons of the 1960s.

Development took place over four years and cost £6 million, a considerable investment for a small firm ploughing through the credit squeeze years of the late 1960s. Ever-changing international regulations extended great influence, particularly in Jaguar's all-important American market. An added complication was indecision on which power unit to use: the well tried 4.2-litre XK engine, a 3-litre unit (with the same straight six, twin overhead camshaft configuration, but developed from one of the racing engines of the late 1950s) or their new twelve-cylinder, which had been under development since the early 1960s. Nor were they certain exactly what shape the twelve-cylinder engine should take: a bulky, but ultra-powerful four overhead cam V12 like those used in the best Italian exotic cars, or a simpler two overhead cam V12. Eventually they plumped for the two overhead cam unit, detailed in Chapter Three.

Inevitably, these factors were reflected in the development of the chassis. Progress on the new two ohc twelve-cylinder engine was slow, so a straight six had to be used initially. But room would be needed for the twelve-cylinder when it became available. Hence the XJ's wide engine bay and bonnet. The basic integral body and chassis unit followed the practice adopted for the 420 and 420G saloons. (Earlier big Jaguars had a separate chassis.) But the suspension was a simplified version of that used on the 420s and the E type. Instead of having a massively substantial rear subframe bolted via rubber blocks into the bodyshell, the suspension units were bolted directly on to the body.

The rear suspension itself was virtually the same as that on the earlier cars, with a single bottom wishbone and the half shaft forming the upper link. The only difference, in experimental layouts fitted to hack Mark 10 (or 420G) saloons, was the torque tube, linked to the solidly mounted differential casing. This meant that the familiar location, by twin trailing arms, could be abandoned.

The hack saloons fitted with the experimental back suspension handled perfectly well, but they boomed, eventually forcing the chassis engineers to revert to the old-established layout. Actually, it was quite some time before they realized that the rear suspension mountings were responsible for the noise, and during that time concentrated on remounting the exhaust system. This method of damping bad vibrations proved so successful that they retained the new exhaust mountings— which were really reinforced rubber bands—on production models.

The front suspension was on the same principle as in previous models, but the mountings were further refined. A large box section member carried the front wishbones and the engine. Road noise was thus reduced because the weight of the engine was concentrated over the front wheels rather than slightly further back with a torsional member in between. The extra weight meant that the front suspension had to incorporate anti-dive geometry; as a bonus, it was possible to soften the coil springs, with a consequent improvement in ride.

At the same time it was possible to improve the

Bob Knight, appointed Managing Director of Jaguar Cars in 1978, whose charge it is to keep the marque at the top into the 1980s

Left *The car that begat the XJ; Jaguar's bulbous Mark 10 of 1962 which provided performance and luxury at a low cost*

Below *The Jaguar Mark 10 developed into the 420G which continued in production alongside the XJ until there was space for it no more*

steering, using a rack and pinion like that on the E type and later-series XK sports cars and dropping the 'varying ratio' idea used on the 420s. In theory, the XJ should have felt like a sports car, and went a long way towards it. But, unfortunately, Jaguar decided to opt for a light setting for the rack's power assistance—to please the American market—and critical comments (from

Jaguars made a number of mock-ups on the way to evaluating the final XJ shape. This is a very early effort—certainly a non-runner—the origins of which have been lost in the mists of time but it is evident from this head-on view that the front bumper came from a Jaguar Mark 10, air intake embellishment from an E type series one (dating the prototype at probably pre-1964) with bonnet and wings made by modifying an E type centre panel pressing and the tops of Mark 10 or S type wings. Contrary to immediate impressions, the windscreen is not split. The central strut is needed to hold the roof up!

the Press rather than the customer) about lack of feel in the steering continue to this day. Ninety-nine per cent of all XJs carry the 'optional' power steering, although some, particularly the odd police-specification car, do not.

Throughout the years, Jaguars had always been on the limit of their braking performance, such was the speed of which they were capable.

The triple-pot Girling calipers were fitted at the front to reduce fade and prolong pad life. The inboard rear disc brakes retained the well-tried twin-pot calipers with separate handbrake. The only real problem here is that hard-used examples generate so much heat that oil seals suffer on the adjacent final drive unit. It certainly pays to keep an eye on an XJ's brakes, although, properly maintained, they are perfectly adequate.

With the 1968 launch date fast approaching, a decision had been taken to adopt the two

A side view of the pop-rivet special shows more clearly where the bits and pieces came from. The rear end is obviously part of a series one E type, grafted on to a Jaguar S type chassis pan

overhead camshaft V12 engine when it could be introduced on the XJ. At last the shape of the engine bay could be finalized and a six-cylinder 4.2-litre engine was installed in the first prototype. As an immediate solution to the problem of projecting cam covers, the characteristic bulge in the centre of the XJ's bonnet arrived. Much time and energy was spent on improving the engine's cooling system by redesigning the water pump and water passages, to counteract claims from America that all Jaguars boiled over in traffic jams. These modifications were entirely successful.

A smaller-engined version was also visualized for potential customers more interested in economy than ultimate performance. Its capacity was eventually settled at 2.8 litres because that was the barrier over which European taxation regulations made a car much more expensive to run

(BMW and Mercedes-Benz subsequently also marketed 2.8-litre cars in recognition of this fact). The engine was based on the earlier 2.4-litre unit, used as an option in the medium-sized saloons. It was made as powerful as possible, however, by equipping it with a straight port head identical to that of the 4.2-litre, and with the bore and stroke almost equal it could be revved harder.

All the Jaguar mock-ups and early prototypes had wire wheels, and Bill Heynes's personal car always had them. Eventually, however, the production cars received steel wheels in the interests of economy. In the background are Jaguar S type bodyshells and in the air inside the factory, a Jaguar Mark II shell

A prototype XJ under test showing the vain attempts to disguise its final form with masking tape

This is one of the first batch of demonstration cars built in 1968. It led a sheltered life, however, as the 2·8-litre version of the XJ6 were not normally released for road testing by the Press as Jaguars naturally preferred comments on the higher-performance 4·2-litre model

Unfortunately, most early examples suffered from holed pistons under certain conditions, possibly due to the dubious quality of the metal used. If the car was driven gently for a period—say, a couple of months pottering around town—and then hammered up a motorway, the pistons went ping. This was because the carbon, which had gradually built up on the pistons, caused detonation when the car was driven hard. Factory experimental testers never encountered this problem on prototypes because they hammered them everywhere, keeping the engines clean! These problems, and an inferior performance, particularly with automatic models, meant that the 2.8-litre XJ6 was never a popular car. Many people bought them early in the XJ6's production life, however, because they were the only example of the model generally available, such was the demand for any XJ6.

The car was such a bargain: it was superior in almost every department to anything else on the road, yet cost only £1797 (in Britain) in its most basic 2.8-litre form and £2397 with the most

One of the original Press loan cars, an overdrive model, later used by Andrew Whyte from 1972 to 1974

desirable options—a 4.2-litre engine and automatic transmission. Times had obviously changed for Jaguar Cars—their previous medium-sized saloons were considered most desirable with a manual gearbox and overdrive! A Mercedes-Benz equivalent, the 300 SEL, generally cost more than twice as much and a Rolls-Royce Silver Shadow was simply exorbitant. No wonder there was an instant black market with 'used' XJ6s fetching £1000 over list price. The ultra-critical *CAR* magazine promptly gave it their Car of the Year award; *CAR*'s international panel of fifteen experienced testers and analysts from seven countries had recognized that this unique car embodied hidden qualities that set it apart from its competitors all over the world. These qualities—particularly of ride and roadholding—more than counterbalance the attractions of contenders which may be cheaper, better looking, faster or more universal in their appeal. They are sufficient to outweigh the fact that, in a sense, the Jaguar is not even more complete! Obviously, they were anticipating the XJ12 to come. . . .

23

Chapter 2
Was the '6' Enough?

Crash testing at the Motor Industry Research Association's establishment at Nuneaton for the American market has become one of the vital necessities for British cars—which is why the XJ6 on the right has a somewhat modified nose. Despite the severity of the impact, the design of the shell has allowed the front to crumple progressively, leaving the passenger compartment unscathed

A new Jaguar is always an event of major significance in the motoring world and few cars have been awaited with greater interest than the XJ6, which was announced on 26 September, 1968. The three models listed—the standard 2.8, the 2.8 de luxe and the 4.2—were the most refined, safest and advanced saloons ever produced by Jaguars. Such was the demand that very few standard 2.8 saloons were made and all them had the 'optional' power steering as standard!

The new body was slightly longer (1.25 in, 32 mm) and noticeably wider (3 in, 76 mm) and lower (1.5 in, 38 mm) than the previous 420; a much better-looking car. Individual armchair-style front seats were a big improvement in that they held the driver and passenger securely. The one-piece back seat had a fold-down centre rest, except on the rare 2.8 standard model. This also had Ambla upholstery rather than the leather used on the 2.8 de luxe and the 4.2. The only other notable differences were a more spartan console with an open tray for oddments rather than a lidded box, and the omission of a rear heater duct.

The heating system had occupied a great deal of development time at the Jaguar factory. It was completely new, incorporating face-level variable-direction and volume air ducts of the type pioneered by Ford with their Cortina. In

As soon as the first batch of early production cars were off the stocks, they were whisked away for publicity pictures such as that below

addition, automatic temperature control was provided by a heat sensor, operated by a multi-setting regulator on the console. Extractor vents, hidden from outside by the bootlid, were fitted below the rear window and avoided the necessity of opening the rear quarter lights as on earlier Jaguar saloons. Opening front quarter lights were retained in the belt-and-braces British tradition, but the real idea was to eliminate potential sources of wind noise.

Noise had become something of an obsession with Jaguar when they were developing the XJ6. They wanted to make it as quiet, or even quieter, than a Rolls-Royce, and—more important—some of their American rivals' cars, such as Cadillac. Anybody who has ever travelled in an XJ6 will testify that they were really successful. One key to the XJ's quietness lies in the mounting of the engine on the front subframe, which, in effect, doubles the insulation between engine and passen-

Press demonstrations followed thick and fast with this left-hand-drive XJ6 being put through its paces on a racing circuit

ger compartment. To illustrate the work which went on in this quest for a truly quiet car, William Heynes points out that there are six different mixes of natural or synthetic rubber in the front suspension and subframe mountings, each with a different frequency characteristic. It was quite a problem to ensure that these predetermined characteristics were maintained within reasonable tolerances in supplies for the production line. In the early stages the development engineers had put prototype cars on vibrators to research the resonances at different frequencies. Everything had to be duplicated in view of the alternative engines, so the final battle was waged on preproduction cars built entirely on production tooling. The hand-built prototypes were not sufficiently representative.

The intensity with which they attacked 'road-excited body noise' was exemplified by the brief given to Dunlop, who developed the XJ's magnificent tyres. Jaguars asked for as much grip and handling as possible; leave the problem of noise to us. Dunlop—who had had some great seasons in Formula One racing—were world leaders in wet-weather grip at the time and well up to their rivals in the dry. As a bonus they designed their E70VR15 tyres for the XJ with a circumferentially irregular tread pattern to break up possible resonances. They were not the quietest of tyres, but they represented great progress in that direction. Jaguar's chief rivals, Mercedes-Benz, took the opposite approach with their 230/250 range. They chose their tyres specifically for quietness and ride and then looked to a sophisticated suspension to make their cars handle well. In a direct comparison between the cars, Jaguar won convincingly, with the XJ outhandling and outriding the Mercedes with greatly reduced noise levels. Development chief Bob Knight was

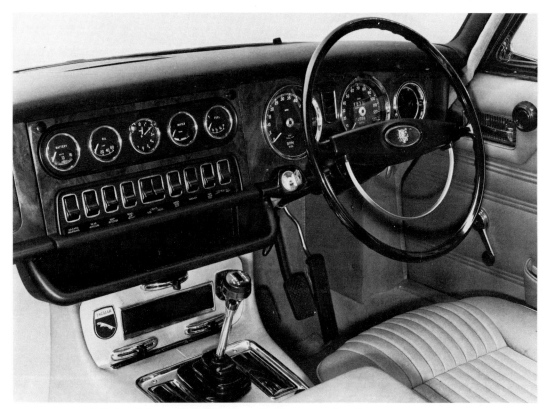

so successful in his attempts to damp out bad vibrations that Jaguar were able to take advantage of the Dunlop radial ply tyres' superior roadholding qualities, while Rolls-Royce were stuck with old-fashioned cross-ply tyres for four more years.

Further sources of noise were reduced by increasing the helix angle of the manual transmission's gears from 29 degrees 30 minutes to 34° 33' for the third gear cluster—not forgetting the cardboard tube rammed inside the propeller shaft! What a constrast in sophisticated engineering and back-street dodging. But Jaguar didn't care how they cut back on noise so long as their methods worked.

The neat, traditional, dashboard and interior of the Jaguar XJ6 was well received on its launch in 1968. The design went a long way to making people feel that the new XJ6 still had the Jaguar touch before they even turned its starting switch

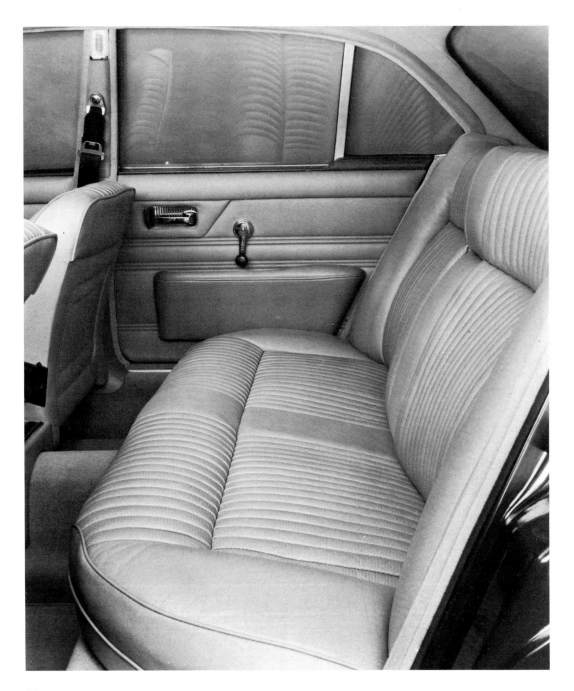

The problem of wind noise was attacked with comparable sophistication. Being already well in advance of other volume car makers with aerodynamicist Malcolm Sayer's E type, Jaguar got it right with the XJ. Because the XJ was a saloon car in which weight was not of prime importance, they were able to pay more effective attention to sealing and sound deadening. Body panels were covered with bitumen-impregnated fibreboard and the entire floor area, which included the luggage boot and propeller shaft tunnel, was covered with snugly fitting thick felt. Even the box section members at the rear door opening were filled with padding to absorb road noise. Finally the entire underside of the body was treated with a rubber-based underseal, which deadened the noise as well as protecting the body.

Safety was another major consideration in the design of the XJ. Sir William Lyons started sketching the XJ's outline in 1962, a year after America had taken serious note of lawyer Ralph Nader's attack on the Chevrolet Corvair in his book *Unsafe At Any Speed*. Sir William recognized the impending shift of opinion and realized that his new saloon had to be super-safe. By the time the basic design was frozen and development started in 1964, safety studies were reaching a peak.

Jaguar had always tried to produce 'safe' cars, concentrating on the primary aspects of avoiding an accident. Jaguar was the first company to investigate and develop to production standard such basic features as four-wheel disc brakes, high-speed tyres for everyday use, ball-pin location of front wheels for much improved steering accuracy and the monocoque principles of body construction as applied to medium-volume passenger cars. Efficient suspension control was developed on both the race track and the simulated

The broad back seat of the XJ6 could be divided by lowering an arm rest in the middle. Note the arm-rest-cum-cubbyhole on the inside of the rear door, which made an ideal base for a multi-speaker stereo system

31

The XJ6 in its initial stages of production at Brown's Lane before the basic shell had received engine, transmission and suspension units

No matter how long the twin overhead camshaft six-cylinder XK engine had been in production, it was still meticulously bench tested

road proving grounds. Now their engineers turned to the secondary aspects of road safety, such as minimizing the risks involved to a passenger when a car crashes.

The centre section of the XJ bodyshell was made as strong as possible with massive box-section side members, scuttle and rear seat pan assemblies. In relation to this section, the front

34

and rear assemblies were less rigid. Thus the bodyshell absorbed impacts from front or rear by crumpling, leaving the passenger area intact. The strong side members and doors not only helped rigidity, so necessary in a good-handling car with soft suspension such as the XJ, but helped protect the occupants in the event of a side impact. All four doors were mounted on very rigid hinges and burst-proof door locks were fitted as standard with child-proof locks at the back. In addition, the location of the engine and transmission unit in relation to the scuttle assembly was such that, should the engine be displaced in an accident, it would be deflected downwards and away from the passenger compartment.

The fuel system came in for particular attention. The fuel pipes were routed well away from potential sources of impact and the twin 11.5-gallon tanks were once again enclosed in their own compartments in the rear wings. Also, the fuel fillers were recessed into the bodywork and

One of the keys to Jaguar's success in making the XJ such a comfortable and good-looking car: the rear suspension unit viewed from the front

the quick action caps fitted with flush release buttons to prevent accidental opening and consequent spillage in the event of a crash. The brakes were fitted with separate hydraulic circuits front and rear in case one failed. The steering rack was mounted on the rear face of the suspension beam for maximum safety and the steering column was fitted with energy-absorbing links and universal joints to cushion the impact of the steering wheel on the driver's body in a severe crash. Front seats were given extremely rigid mountings and padded at the back to protect rear-seat passengers, should they be thrown forward, while reinforced seat-belt anchorages were fitted front and rear.

The interior was redesigned on established Jaguar lines, but with the following safety features: the instrument panel was fitted with an energy-absorbing surround; the traditional toggle and rotary light switches were replaced by the rocker type; the old ignition key and push button starter were replaced by a combined ignition and steering lock on the steering column, out of the way of arms and legs; softly padded sun visors were fitted with a breakaway anti-dazzle interior mirror; wheel-operated front quarter lights were introduced with the slim-line window winders on non-electric window cars; and a matt finish was put on metal parts likely to cause dazzle by reflection.

Further safety aspects included large-area side-lamps and flashers, which were visible from the side; a comprehensive electrical fusing system; a hazard-warning system allowing all four indicators to be switched on, and a large window area for maximum all-round visibility.

The American motoring magazine *Road & Track*, champion of the imported sporting car, summed it all up when large numbers of XJs

The independent front suspension of the XJ was almost completely new, having been mounted with a sub-frame—visible on the left of the picture—on rubber to absorb shocks and road noise. The damper's new mounting outside the coil spring can be seen clearly

started arriving in America in 1970 by saying: 'The new Jaguar is uncannily swift, gloriously silent and as safe as houses'.

Jaguars had always been 'uncannily swift' since the introduction of the XK engine in 1948. Although this engine was years ahead of its time then, twenty years of development (and more than 250,000 units made by 1968) had increased its power and torque to gross 245 bhp (SAE) at 6000 rpm and 182 lb/ft at 3750 rpm for the 2.8-litre Both engines had the alloy cylinder head of the E type sports car. The cast-iron cylinder block followed established XK practice with a forged steel crankshaft running in seven large-diameter bearings—almost indestructible! Years of production also ensured that this straight six-cylinder engine was so reliable that overhauls were rarely necessary before less than 80,000 miles. Twin SU HD8 two-inch carburettors with automatic choke were fitted on non-American specification cars (American XJs had twin Zenith Stromberg 175 CDs) rather than the three carburettors of the E type. This kept fuel consumption to 15–20 mpg (Imperial) with the 4.2-litre and 17–22 mpg for the 2.8. Overdrive models usually managed about three mpg more than automatics, because of the power absorbed by the automatic gearbox's torque converter.

Manual transmission cars used Jaguar's four-speed box with overdrive as a 'standard' option; non-overdrive XJs are distinct oddities. The all-synchromesh gearbox's ratios were: first 3.04:1; second 1.97; third 1.33; and fourth direct with a twenty-eight per cent reduction in engine speed when the Laycock overdrive was engaged by a new gearlever-mounted switch. Much later, XJs were fitted with a new five-speed gearbox, described later in this chapter. Early automatic cars were fitted with the Borg Warner type 35 box on

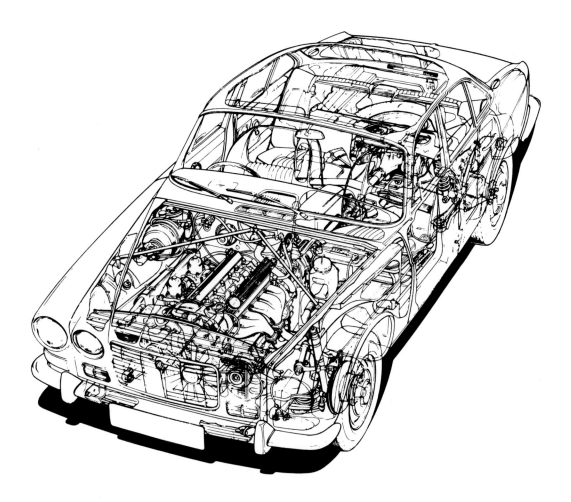

the 2.8, and the Model 8 Borg Warner on the 4.2. A transmission oil heat-exchanger in the bottom of the water radiator was used on both models. These units were used extensively on other Jaguar cars, but the type 35 gearbox had a different method of operation on the 2.8-litre. It had a 'D, 2, 1' control system enabling all three ratios to be used in D (for drive), or just the lower two in 2, with 1 as a hold in the first gear only. Thus a measure of manual selection could be used

Cutaway drawing of the XJ6 saloon showing the location of its major components

39

that was helpful particularly when driving fast over winding roads or descending steep hills. The 4.2 cars fitted with the Model 8 transmission had a similar system, using D1 and D2 on their selector. When D1 was engaged, all three gears were used for maximum acceleration; when D2 was engaged only the top two gears were used for maximum smoothness on take-off; there was also an L for lock-up, or holding the first gear, or for changing down from the third gear to second. Both installations also, in theory, featured a part-throttle downshift enabling the driver to change down by pressing the accelerator pedal without having to go past full throttle, as on the earlier 'kickdown' system. This made gearchanging much smoother.

Rear axle ratios for the hypoid differential unit were 4.27:1 on the 'non-overdrive' and automatic 2.8; 4.55 on the overdrive 2.8; 3.77 on the overdrive 4.2. The differential unit was mounted with its inboard back brakes on the subframe at the rear of the car.

The suspension was designed so that, when cornering, the outer rear wheel—which carries the main cornering forces—remained vertical to the road. This was considered vital with such wide tyres. The system consisted of a lower transverse tubular link on each side, pivoted at the wheel carrier and subframe with the universally jointed half shaft as the upper link. Longitudinal location was by 'vee' rubber mountings locating the sub-assembly in the body structure and by radius arm each side between the lower link and the body. Twin coil springs each side, each enclosing a telescopic damper, provided the suspension medium. This subframe was easily detachable from the body, and its rubber mountings were designed to give a compliance of 5 degrees around the centre of gravity of the differential unit under acceleration and 3 degrees under braking. These limits were carefully calculated to eliminate as much noise and transmission harshness as possible without detracting too much from the roadholding.

The front suspension was largely new. It used unequal-length transverse wishbones with coil springs, telescopic dampers and a 0.675-inch (17.1 mm) anti-roll bar. The springs were located between the lower wishbones and turrets, which were part of the suspension subframe. This meant that all shocks, and noise, were fed through the subframe's rubber mountings. The subframe also made the assembly easy to remove and refit. The dampers were positioned—contrary to previous Jaguar practice—outside the coil spring. With the suspension's anti-dive geometry and subsequently soft springs, it was an important factor in achieving the XJ's good ride and roadholding because it allowed more damper travel.

The steering was also a new design for Jaguar, developed in close conjunction with Adwest. The rack and pinion, which gave 3.5 turns from lock to lock of the 36-foot (10.97 m) turning circle, was of exceptionally precise manufacture. This meant that a high level of power assistance could be used and was the reason why, once confidence had been established in the XJ's very light steering, it was possible to drive it as fast as a car with heavier, easier-to-feel steering.

Such was the XJ's reception that a year-long waiting list quickly established itself with substantial premiums needed to jump the queue. Jaguars carried on with the 420 in Daimler Sovereign guise until August 1969 before introducing the Daimler version of the XJ on 9 October, 1969. This was exactly the same as the Jaguar XJ6 except that it had the traditional Daimler fluted radiator grille, special badges and a number of extras, some 'compulsory' such as

One of the few differences between the new Daimler Sovereign saloon introduced in 1969 and the Jaguar XJ6 was its distinctive radiator grille

overdrive, incorporated as standard. It was available only in de luxe 2.8 and 4.2 form and not at all in America, which started receiving their XJ6s in quantity late in 1970 when the model had passed their stringent safety checks. America took only 4.2-litre cars and they were called, simply, the XJ sedan.

Jaguar 420G production was axed in August

1970 and helped provide space for more XJs to be built. Production of the Daimler limousine, based on the 420G, continued at the Vanden Plas works in London. It had little in common with the XJ other than some running gear and detail fittings.

Detail improvements were made constantly while the XJ was in production. The front suspension was stiffened a little in 1969 and tyre

The interior of the Daimler Sovereign followed closely on that of the Jaguar XJ6. This is a rare non-electric window version. Daimlers with a manual gearbox were even rarer

clearance improved by new front wheel arches in October 1970; optional head rests were offered from August 1969 with inertia reel seat belts. Heat shields were fitted between the body and exhaust in November 1969; door locks were improved, footwell vents added, the scuttle vent grille changed from dazzling chrome to satin finish and non-reflective bezels fitted to the instruments in spring 1970.

In October, new aluminium door tread plates were fitted, incorporating the name Jaguar; such had been Sir William's confidence in the identity of the car that the name appeared nowhere else on the body! No doubt this was tolerated because there was now a Daimler version. Lyons had the right to confidence in his car's distinctive appearance; his styling ability was so good that the Jaguar's square radiator grille—which had looked plain nasty in similar form on a Studebaker Lark—was entirely in sympathy with the overall XJ shape. Unfortunately, although the Daimler grille looked impressive, it did not fit in quite so well as the original.

Quieter-running camshafts were fitted to all XK engines from November 1969, engine mountings improved and US exhaust emission-type manifolds standardized in March 1970. The old type of XK camshaft sprocket adjuster with vernier teeth in place of lobes was reintroduced (and fitted retrospectively) when it was found the lobes could strip, with disastrous results for the valve gear. In the summer of 1970 a new brake fluid reservoir was fitted in front of the servo and an improved crankshaft oil seal fitted to the 2.8 from April 1971.

Sidelights and flashers were altered to meet European regulations in March 1970 and rear lights in August 1970. A three-piece rear bumper was fitted in March 1971 to reduce repair costs, already minimized by the use of bolt-on rear under panels and front wings.

The most significant change, however, was in the 4.2's automatic gearbox. During the first six months of 1970 it was updated to the Borg Warner Model 12 (the 2.8's model 35 was already reasonably up to date). This was a much tougher gearbox that had the bonus of allowing acceleration almost on a par with that of a manual 4.2, which returned 0–60 mph (97 km/h) times of 8.8 seconds; earlier 4.2 automatics took around 10 seconds (the 2.8 automatic took 12.6 seconds and the manual equivalent 11 seconds). The new gearbox also worked well in conjunction with the 3.31 axle ratio which had been fitted to all 4.2 models other than those destined for North America in August 1969 (the 2.8 got a 4.09 axle at the same time).

Weekly production was increased steadily to around 650 XJs, 100 of them going to North America, and a total of fifty-six per cent being exported. Gradually the waiting list was reduced, although it was to be a long time before it came down to a few weeks, as the new XJ12 (the subject of the next chapter) was about to be introduced.

The press had a preview of the first long-wheelbase version of the XJ12, a Daimler Double-Six Vanden Plas, in July 1972 and it was introduced as optional on all models, including the XJ6, in October 1972. An extra four inches (102 mm) of wheelbase made the rear passengers' compartment seem a lot roomier and was the result of a sudden decision following the successful marketing of more spacious Mercedes-Benz saloons (the SEL as opposed to SE). It added an extra 170 pounds (77 kg) to the existing rather heavy weight of close on 3500 pounds (1590 kg). Sixty miles an hour from rest took about 0.5 seconds longer and petrol consumption was in-

An optional long wheelbase shell was offered on Jaguar and Daimler models from 1972. It had an extra four inches let into the rear passenger compartment to make it more competitive with a new Mercedes-Benz SEL range

The extra inches in the back of the long-wheelbase XJs were reflected in the much-improved leg room, emphasised by the front seats in the picture above at full stretch forward and backward

creased by about 1 mpg, but handling and ride were just as good. The new model was called the XJ6L. By then, 2.8-litre production was minimal owing to lack of demand (everybody wanted an XJ12 or 4.2-litre XJ6) and that model ceased production in April 1973.

The next big change was the introduction of the series II XJs at the Frankfurt Motor Show on 13 September, 1973. Vigorous attempts were made to meet criticisms (mostly minor) which had been levelled at the earlier cars, with the exception of the steering, which remained as light as ever. These series II cars were shown with a new two-door model called the XJ6C or XJ12C (for coupé), which used the shorter-wheelbase floorpan, al-

though there was no intention of starting coupé production until early 1974 as there was still some development to be done. In the event, regular production did not get going until early 1975. Daimler equivalents of each variation were also produced.

The most noticeable difference between the series II and earlier cars was in the frontal appearance and interior. A new bumper bar was raised to sixteen inches (406 mm) from the ground to meet American regulations, which demanded that bumper heights should be standardized; they were rather a waste of time and money for most cars as it happened, because, in an accident, heavy braking tends to depress the nose of a car

A Jaguar XJ6 version of the long-wheelbase saloon showing the extra width available in the rear door openings

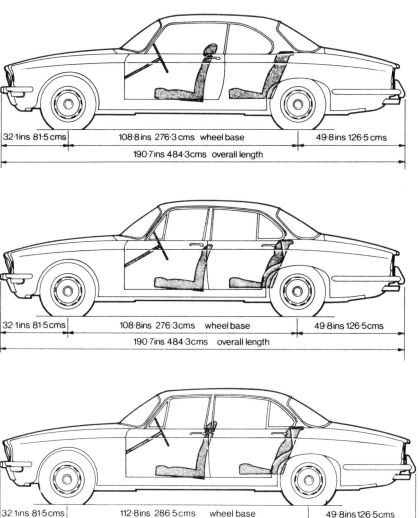

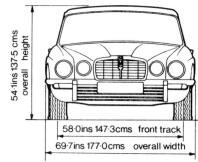

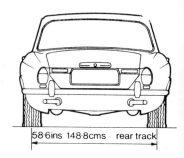

The three versions of the series two XJ planned by Jaguars in 1973: top, the short-wheelbase coupé; middle, a short-wheelbase saloon; and bottom, the long-wheelbase saloon, with front and rear aspects at the right of the drawing. In the event, the short-wheelbase saloon never went into production and production of the coupé was long delayed by development problems

and raise the back (not to the full extent with the XJ's anti-dive suspension), meaning that there can be a difference of up to twelve inches (300 mm) between front and rear bumpers on impact, even when they are of the same static height. Something the rule-makers, if not the car-makers, forgot.

The subtle differences between Daimler and Jaguar versions of the XJ including the Daimler's grille on the left and the Jaguar's on the right

The revised interior of the series two XJ6 showing the new heating and ventilation unit and relocated gauges

The radiator grilles and lighting were re-arranged to allow for this and redesigned at the back to meet new regulations.

The interior was extensively modified: leather and walnut were still in ample evidence, but now all the instruments were grouped in front of the driver, visible through a heavily padded 'safety'

steering wheel. Switches were rearranged around this display and a grille for a new heating/air conditioning unit occupied the dashboard's centre. (Old-style air conditioning had been available as an option on 4.2 models.) Other controls, such as the dip-switch on the floor, were transferred to steering column stalks. Electric

Federal versions of the 1973 XJ6 bound for America could be readily identified by their sidelights and reinforced bumpers

What might have been; a prototype of the series two short-wheelbase XJ saloon

Relatively simple and uncomplicated! The 1974 European specification XK engine installation

windows were standardized, as was the longer wheelbase on four-door cars and the ventilated front brake discs introduced on the E type in 1971.

A central locking system, operated by solenoids, was fitted for the doors and a cut-out switch to stop children playing with the window lifts.

The floppy and inadequate 'safety' parcel shelf beneath the dashboard was replaced with a

passenger's glove box of far more useable size than before. The front door armrests were enlarged and grab handles became easier to grab. The central rear ashtray was replaced by ashtrays in each door because the previous ventilation system had tended to blow ash in people's faces.

It was the first British production car to use fibre-optic lighting cable—a sort of flexible strip light—on the instruments, which eliminated a

The XJ coupé photographed in prototype form in September 1973 showing the long unbroken window line favoured by Sir William Lyons

57

variety of bulbs, saving space. A heated rear window, laminated windscreen, head restraints and inertia reel seat belts became standard fittings.

The heating and ventilation unit was innovatory. It operated on air-blending principles rather than on a water-valve control as before. Instant changes in temperature became possible and a set temperature could be maintained regardless of outside influences. The heater was also made more powerful, and air conditioning boosted to an output of 300 cubic feet (8.5 m³) per minute instead of 200 cubic feet (5.6 m³), to stop Americans getting hot under the collar. Jaguar's engineers went to the Arctic and Arizona to find out what it was all about—and not before time!

The front bulkhead had to be redesigned to accommodate this new, larger unit. This meant that the bulkhead could have only one skin, instead of a box section, and might therefore be less resistant to the penetration of heat and noise from the engine compartment. Jaguar avoided this possibility by fitting a full-width asbestos shield on the engine side of the bulkhead with bitumen, felt and foam covering on the passenger side. The pedal and steering column openings were sealed with flexible boots. Sockets similar to those used on caravan connections (and the E type bonnet) were used so that wiring did not have to pass through grommets, which have a tendency to fall out and do not seal well in any case. Piping was connected via tubes fixed in the bulkhead to which individual hoses could be connected on either side. All this made the car easier to service as pipes and wiring could be detached independently from either side of the bulkhead.

Mechanically, the cars were little changed except that the engine had a new air cleaner and thermostatically controlled exhaust-heated air

Frontal aspect of the XJ6 coupé with little to identify the difference between that and the saloon car apart from the window line on the right

intake system, which reduced power to 170 bhp (DIN) at 4500 rpm. A new single-tube oil cooler was fitted and an extended downpipe replaced the notoriously unreliable flexible section in the exhaust system. The doors received extra internal bracing to meet American side-impact regulations.

The new two-door was Sir William Lyon's last fling before he retired in 1972. It took so long to get into production because of problems with sealing and mechanizing the rear windows.

The coupé was based on the short-wheelbase XJ. Its doors were four inches (101.6 mm) longer than the normal front doors, which were, incidentally, the same length on both short- and long-wheelbase variants. Extra length in the latter was taken up in the rear doors. The central pillar was removed and the rear door shutpost

reinforced. A wider rear pillar, disguised by a black, grained vinyl roof covering, made for extra strength. Both front and rear windows were arranged so that they could be wound down out of sight, presenting a stunning side profile. The rear windows, therefore, had to tilt to miss the wheel arches, which indirectly had the disconcerting effect that they could easily be sucked out because they were in a low-pressure area. An unacceptable level of wind noise resulted, eventually overcome by Jaguar with a tensioned pulley arrangement.

The whole structure, sufficiently rigid to meet Jaguar's own high standards, could not, however, survive American impact regulations, so the car could not be sold there. This was one of the reasons why it was produced only in small numbers, and accounted for its demise in early 1978. Other reasons were that it could not be made in large

The Jaguar XJ 3·4-litre saloon introduced in April 1975

quantities, it did not sell well in the 'executive' market place, the problem of continuing wind noise (although this could be 'adjusted out' by experts), the obsolete floor pan used and the fact that factory space was needed to meet the demand for four-door cars. Even so, it has been hailed as a classic of styling and was slightly faster and more economical than the four-door cars because it was lighter. Perhaps if the car had been played 'up market' it would have succeeded—it even shared sales brochures with the saloons.

Production of the XJ6s continued unabated during 1973 and 1974 as it became apparent that the six-cylinder engine had a much better future than the twelve-cylinder during the newly recognized world energy shortage. Therefore, in April 1975, a 3.4-litre economy version of the four-door XJ6 was introduced—a replacement for the 2.8. This model used the dimensions of 83 mm bore and 106 mm stroke made famous by the original XK engine, which had continued in production with the 340 model until that had to give way to the XJ6 in September 1968. The basic layout and size might have been the same, but the cylinder block was different. Power steering was hailed at the same time as 'standard' on all XJs, at last!

The new block was similar to that of the 4.2-litre with offset bores and the same head and carburettors, all of which helped keep down costs. Manual with overdrive or Borg Warner Model 65 automatic transmission could be specified with a common 3.54 final drive ratio. The all-important fuel consumption was reduced to 17–21 mpg on manual versions. (It must be remembered that the new 3.4-litre XJ6 used the by now much heavier series II shell, whereas the earlier XJ6 benefited from a lighter weight.) A comparison of the performance figures is interesting: the early XJ6s were capable of 123 mph (198 km/h) with a 0–60

time of more than two seconds better than the XJ6 3.4's 10.9; however, by 1975 the XJ6 4.2 had been slowed down by a reduction in compression ratio and other changes necessary to meet American emission regulations. The chief difference in performance, other than in fuel consumption, was a loss in top gear acceleration and flexibility, with the 3.4 manual taking 9.5 seconds to accelerate from 30 to 50 mph (48 to 80 km/h) against the 4.2 equivalent's 6.9 seconds.

Economies were made in the 3.4's interior to help keep the cost down to £4794 against the 4.2's

The complex underbonnet view of the 1978 US Jaguar XK engine showing its feedback-controlled fuel injection and three-way catalyst

*Unashamed luxury; the
Daimler Vanden Plas 4·2-
litre saloon showing its
distinctive chrome side
flashes*

*Far right MWK 22G, chassis
IL 1006 DN was the sixth
right hand drive XJ6 made
and the first with overdrive
photographed here in Glen
Lyon in Northern Scotland*

Above *MVC 203G from the
rear en route to Turin in
October 1968 near Vitteaux.
One of the original six rhd
works XJs, IL 1003 BW, later
converted to 'DN'*

Right *One of the first Jaguar
XJ12s, a works demonstrator*

Above right *Daimler's
Double Six at its Swiss
launch in 1972*

Far right *Series II Jaguar
XJ12L. A works
demonstrator*

Left *A most striking shot of a privately-owned XJ-S of 1976 vintage*

Top *Ex-works XJ12C Group 2 racing saloon as it is today*

Below *A very early left-hand drive XJ6C en route to Milan in 1974*

Left *A special Avon bodied XJ convertible, one of two or more examples currently available in the UK, stands next to Andrew Whyte's unique ex-works press demonstrator XJ4.2C which has had its vinyl roof removed and lower grille simplified. Perhaps the most beautiful XJ of all?*

Above *The Pininfarina designed XJ Spider based on the XJ-S was shown at both the Turin and Birmingham Motor Shows in 1978. Will it be produced at Coventry?*

Series III Jaguar XJ 4.2
clearly shows off its
increased rear headroom yet
confirms the very 'rightness'
of the basic twelve year old
design

£5136 at the time of the first 3.4. The seats were given cloth-trimmed facing which could also be specified in the 4.2, when they came with matching door panels. At the same time, all XJs were modified to improve the handling still further. These changes included revision of the steering rack, anti-roll bar, castor angle, steering arms and wishbones. And a new Daimler using the XJ12 (or Daimler Double Six) Vanden Plas body was listed with a 4.2-litre engine—a sort of economy/luxury version of the XJ6.

These Vanden Plas Daimler 'XJs' were built on the normal production line at Coventry, where they received their first colour coat of paint. In this state they were driven to London, where any defects were rectified. On arrival, the vinyl roof was covered with a glass fibre protector and the chrome masked. Then a special paint finish was applied and a more luxurious interior with extra electrical equipment fitted. The cost was about ten per cent more than that of standard models.

The next major change to the XJ6 range was the introduction of fuel injection (for the American market) on the 4.2-litre engine in May 1978 to reduce exhaust emissions and to cut fuel consumption. The 3.4, which was not sold in the United States, continued to use SU carburettors. The fuel injection system fitted was the Lucas/Bosch L-jetronic that had been fitted to the twelve-cylinder cars from April 1975. This had the bonus of compensating for some of the power lost to emission regulations, but cost more to maintain and manufacture. Bendix originated the system, which was then developed by Bosch and later adapted by Lucas and Jaguar. A Bosch electric control was at the heart of this set-up, which was worth an extra 2 mpg. A three-way catalytic converter was also fitted to meet the exhaust standards.

The Jaguar XJ 3·4 in series three form showing clearly its raised roofline, black rubber-faced bumpers and new wheels

The installation was so successful that Jaguar were able to raise the compression ratio from 7.4:1 to 8:1 (it had originally been 9:1) and fit larger inlet valves so that the 4.2-litre engine now developed 176 bhp (DIN) against a previous low of 161 bhp. Costs were reduced by the new technique of fitting a single specification engine, whereas different types had been needed for California and the rest of North America before, to meet their

particular different standards.

The injection system was not immediately fitted to non-American cars, but a new five-speed gearbox was announced in May and introduced from October 1978; American XJs continued to be all-automatic as they had always been. This new gearbox weighed slightly less than the old Jaguar four-speed plus overdrive, and was introduced as a rationalization with the Rover saloons for which it had been designed, which were also produced by British Leyland. Performance was slightly more fussy because of lower gearing, but fuel consumption was little affected.

Back in 1964, when the XJ design was 'frozen', Sir William Lyons envisaged a production run of around seven years; that would have given us a

Above left The revised rear quarter of the series three XJ with the rear quarter of the earlier car, above right, for comparison

The revised interior of the series three car, in Daimler Sovereign form

new Jaguar in 1975 with something completely different for the 1980s. The basic strength of the design was evident in how well the XJ survived, selling with so few alterations—and hardly any of them to the styling—for eleven years until a facelift became desirable. A gauge of how inflation has hit car-makers is that it cost Jaguar £6 million to develop the XJ between 1964 and 1968 and £7 million for a facelift amounting to little more than a raised roofline and more luxurious fittings when the series III XJs were introduced in March 1979. Without a doubt, British Leyland would have liked to have a completely new shape for the XJ series, but the cost of developing a new front and back was prohibitive.

Few criticisms had been levelled at the XJ since 1968, but Jaguar tried to eliminate them with, once again, the notable exception of the steering and the exhaust system. In company with practically everything else mechanical, the steering was left alone; the exhaust material was

changed to stainless steel. Substantial alterations were made, however, to raise the roof to a new line designed by Pininfarina. This new roof was less rounded and its pillars more upright. The rear window was flatter, the side glass deeper, and the front quarter lights abandoned. The result was more room and a more spacious feeling in the passenger compartment, with a strikingly different outside appearance, reminiscent in some ways of the BMW 7-series. The raised roofline allowed the fitting of an electrically operated sunroof (the first as a factory-fitted optional in a Jaguar saloon since the Mark IX twenty years earlier). The windscreen and rear window were fitted to the bodyshell by thermal adhesion, thus increasing its rigidity and providing a better seal against leaks. Tinted glass was used on all cars except the 3.4, where it was offered as an option. New flush-fitting doorhandles complied with the safety regulations, as did massive rubber-covered bumpers (these were mounted on 5 mph (8 km/h)

Frontal view of the series three XJ6 emphasizing the neat and tidy way in which Jaguar had blended in the massive bumpers required by the US market

A fascinating experiment by Pininfarina to alter the XJ's classic lines without detracting from its appearance

impact-absorbing beams on North American models). Indicator lights were fitted within the front bumper and fog warning lights let into the rear bumper. The Jaguars received a new vertical-rib grille and the Daimlers kept their old one. The rear light clusters were redesigned to give a larger illumination, with a new numberplate light and boot handle to complement them. The wheels remained the same size, but were given 'funny' trims for a more sporty appearance, This aspect of the car had always niggled certain factions who even considered fitting wire wheels (never optional) to the XJ in the late 1960s.

The only real mechanical change was the standardization of fuel injection on the 4.2 model, but there were extensive alterations to the interior equipment. The 4.2 automatic received an optional electric cruise control and all cars were fitted with a new security locking system, delay switch for the interior lighting, rear window heater and electric radio aerial, quartz halogen

headlights, a briefcase full of tools in the boot, and a more comprehensive set of warning lights. Headlight washers and wipers and an electrically controlled exterior mirror were offered as options.

The interior was remodelled with thick new carpeting, hidden inertia reels for the seat belts, a new steering wheel and clearer instrumentation. The front seats were completely redesigned to incorporate a wide range of lumbar and electric height adjustment. Sound insulation was further improved by the use of vacuum-formed rubber and foam covers for the door panels, bulkhead and propeller shaft tunnel. The new window fittings also helped in this respect.

In these forms, the six-cylinder Jaguar and Daimler XJ range enter the 1980s and seem set for a good run with their successor hardly off the drawing board.

Later experiments by Bertone—on this model shown at the 1978 Birmingham Motor Show—could not be considered so attractive

79

Chapter 3
Or the '12' Too Much?

As soon and the motoring world saw the size of the XJ6's engine bay, they wondered what was to be slipped into it next; Jaguar said that a new engine was on the way in 'about two years', but refused to give any further clues. So speculation mounted as to whether it would be V12 (or even a V8) as it was obvious that they were seeking even more power than the ageing XK could provide. Extensive development work with emission controls caused Jaguar to postpone the launching of the XJ12 several times in the two years, although there was nothing unusual in that, before it eventually appeared in July 1972. By then it had become evident which engine would power the car: Jaguar had already used the E type as a mobile test bed for the V12 from 1971.

The combination of the E type's V12 engine and the XJ6's bodyshell was 'ecstasy on wheels' said *Road & Track*, echoing the thoughts of keen motorists everywhere. Here was a saloon car with excellent roadholding and ride that was capable of 145 mph (233 km/h) and 0–60 mph (97 km/h) in 7.4 seconds, faster than the majority of so-called GT cars costing perhaps three times as much. The only drawback was fuel consumption of between 11 and 14 mpg, but there wasn't an oil shortage in 1972—petrol was cheap and plentiful in Britain and America. In other countries, where it was more expensive, people who could afford to tax

Despite the glamour of the occasion, the Jaguar XJ12 received more attention than any other model on its introduction at the Earls Court Motor Show in 1972

and insure a Jaguar XJ12 could afford the petrol. They could also ignore the shortcomings of a mere 20-gallon (Imperial) petrol capacity. (The XJ12 shared the XJ6's tanks, which had been reduced in size to meet American safety regulations.) There was an immediate waiting list caused partly by a factory strike with black market prices as there had been for the first XJ6s four years before. Only Daimler Double Six Press cars were seen first.

The basic car was little changed from the 4.2-litre XJ6 except for the engine compartment. The front springs were stiffened to take the extra weight of the V12 engine (680 lb/308 kg against 600/272 for the XK). Ventilated front discs were fitted to cope better with the extra weight and performance, and a Kelsey Hayes brake balance valve incorporated in the braking system reduced the tendency for the rear wheels to lock up (it

The legendary XJ12 on introduction in its original short-wheelbase form

distributed pedal pressure equally between front and rear systems at low loads and increased it on the front at higher loads). Dunlop improved the speed rating of the tyres by using the nylon casing from the V12 E type with a steel breaker strip to cater for the XJ12's higher weight. Wheels with better ventilation were also fitted. The XJ6's Borg Warner Model 12 automatic gearbox was used with no alternative transmission, as there was no overdrive available which could cope with the

Dream car in a dream setting: a classical pose for the short-wheelbase XJ12 saloon

V12 engine's mighty torque of 294 ft/lb gross at 3500 rpm.

It was the impressive torque produced by the two overhead camshaft (single cam per head) V12 which had helped sway Jaguar's engineers towards this configuration rather than that of their well-established twin cam (straight) head. During experiments which had begun in the early 1960s, they tried both four overhead cam and two overhead cam V12s and found that the two cam

Rear view of the XJ12 encumbered only by a discreet badge to indicate its enormous extra urge

provided much better torque up to 5000 rpm. It produced less power at the top end, but its 272 bhp (DIN) in eventual production form was quite sufficient. Other factors influencing this decision were that they were much cheaper to produce and took up less space. This was important in an already crowded engine bay, which was to become packed out with ancillaries when emission laws assumed such importance in the late 1960s. Later it became evident that to have squeezed in a four overhead cam version of the V12 would have been impracticable, as the XJ's wide tyres needed space to manoeuvre in a turning circle.

The decision to use twelve cylinders rather than eight was influenced by two major criteria. A

large proportion of Jaguars were sold in the United States, a market dominated by superb V8 engines. Using a V12 would make the Jaguar different, perhaps putting it in the same class as Ferrari and Lamborghini, which was just the sort of image that Sir William Lyons wanted. Also, the V12 was inherently smoother running than a V8 and in this way it would compare very favourably with similar cars from Mercedes-Benz and Rolls-Royce.

The production V12 was developed to a degree from a four overhead camshaft racing unit built with Le Mans in mind. This engine had a capacity of 4991 cc to keep it within the five-litre Le Mans limit and shared some resemblance to the XK

The complex underbonnet lay-out of the XJ12. Note the battery's cooling fan in the top right hand corner of the picture

engine. The bore and stroke was different, however, at 87 × 70 mm, and the inlet valves were mounted at 60 degrees rather than at 70. The inlet ports were also downdraught rather than straight for space reasons. This engine, tested in a mid-engine racing prototype called the XJ13 produced 502 bhp (SAE) at 7600 rpm. Production versions aimed at 330 bhp (SAE), the best output achieved by a full-race XK engine, with a bore and stroke of 90 × 70 mm, giving 5343 cc, and under revised horsepower ratings of 272 bhp (DIN) gave all of that. Fuel injection and carburettors were tried and at one time it seemed that A E Brico electronic fuel injection would be fitted until that firm suddenly changed its mind about production. Test

Left *Skilled fitters at work building Jaguar's twelve-cylinder engine*

Above *The first manifestation of the XJ12 project was a secret mid-engined long-distance sports racing car called the XJ13 that utilized a four overhead cam version of the new power unit. This is the car that Jaguar thought might win at Le Mans—but by the time it was being developed, tyre technology had rendered the chassis obsolete*

engines were also built with cast iron and alloy
cylinder blocks; Jaguars chose the 116 lb (52.6 kg)
lighter alloy block when it was found to be as quiet
as the cast iron version and dissipated the heat
produced much better. Flat cylinder heads were
designed under Walter Hassan's direction by
Coventry Climax, who had been taken over by
Jaguar. These heads were cheaper to produce and
saved weight. Weight and cost were also reduced
by using a single chain camshaft drive, which had

the added advantage of being quieter.

Four Stromberg carburettors like the three used on the late North American 4.2-litre XK engines were fitted outside the 60-degree engine's vee, because of the restricted bonnet height. Lucas electronic ignition was adopted in view of emission regulations.

Assembly of this outstanding new engine—the world's first mass-produced V12—took place in what had six years earlier been the Daimler

The XJ12 in its 1974 American Federal bumper form

The V12 engine with electronic fuel injection as fitted to the XJ 5.3 and Daimler Double Six from May 1975

factory at Radford in the space once occupied by Majestic Major and SP250 body building. Much of the production equipment was automatic and an investment of £3 million was needed. The machinery was designed in the hope that alternative configurations and capacities might be produced with the same equipment, such as V8 and vee or straight sixes.

The new V12 engines were first tried in 420G saloons in 1967 and the biggest problem with installation in the XJ shell was counteracting the extra heat inevitably produced in the smaller air space surrounding the engine. A bigger water

The XJ 5.3 saloon showing its optional alloy wheels

radiator was fitted and the battery needed its own cooling fan! The steering rack and engine mountings were protected by stainless steel guards and the exhaust downpipes were double-skinned to reduce noise and heat.

Little else changed in the car, apart from the mechanical modifications mentioned above. Daimler Sovereign-style armrests were fitted to the XJ12 and the centre console trimmed in black. A 7000 rpm rev counter was fitted. There was a slightly different grille on Jaguar models. Daimlers were called Double Sixes after a highly esteemed prewar model. The XJ12s priced from

Left *The XJ 5.3 interior
revealing the new cloth
trimming that became
available from May 1975*

Above *Timeless elegance: the
Daimler Double Six Vanden
Plas series two saloon*

£3725, offered unrivalled value for money as had
their predecessors, the XJ6s. Even the V12 cost
little more than one-third the price of a Rolls-
Royce Silver Shadow, for instance.

America, with its crash and emission tests, had
to wait longer than Europe for the XJ12 and their
first models in late 1973 were all series II variants.

The XJ12s, Daimler Double Sixes, Vanden Plas and coupés which followed were virtually the same as the six-cylinder engine models. (The only minor variations were listed earlier in this chapter.) Following the first fuel shortage of 1974, when XJ12 sales suffered badly, fuel injection was fitted to the saloons in April 1975, the coupés

The standard series two Jaguar XJ 5.3 saloon complete with optional driver's wing mirror

The 1957 Jaguar XJ 5.3 coupé which was fitted with fuel injection from May 1975 and optional alloy wheels. Note the use of a vinyl head trimming. This was necessary to disguise imperfect roof pressings as the result of cost-conscious tooling for this low-volume model

always being so fitted. This restored the power lost due to essential modifications as emission regulations grew steadily more severe. At the same time fuel consumption was improved to between 13 and 16 mpg. (The system was described in the previous chapter.)

All twelve-cylinder models could be distinguished by the black vinyl roof and chrome side

Dashboard of the 5.3-litre coupé in standard form

strips on the body. Alloy wheels were an option. The higher axle ratio of the V12 coupé, of 3.07 : 1, was fitted to the saloons to save petrol. The engine was also fitted with a new, improved, rear main bearing side seal.

Nothing else changed in the twelve-cylinder saloons until the substitution of a General Motors 400 Hydramatic gearbox early in 1977. This was a

Above *Yet another variation on the XJ theme—the Daimler version of the 5.3-litre coupé*

Right *The stark and well-protected cockpit of a works 5.3-litre racing coupé*

Above *British Leyland made a desperate attempt to take the European Touring Car championship in 1976 and 1977 with the Jaguar XJ 5.3 coupé. Two cars—one of which is pictured above at Silverstone—were prepared for them by the Broadspeed racing concern*

Left *Such was the complexity of the modifications needed to make the coupés competitive that they suffered from a lack of reliability not typical of the standard car. This is the complicated engine installation*

101

Right *Andy Rouse sets fastest time in practice for the 1977 Tourist Trophy race at Silverstone with a wet-sump version of the racing coupé. These cars were so fast that they left everything else standing, but rarely lasted the full distance*

Left *Tim Schenken in a dry-sump version of the coupé, number one, leads Rouse on the first lap of the 1977 TT with the rival BMWs hanging on. However, the German cars outlasted the British hopes to win the race and the championship. They had been developed over a number of years, whereas there simply was not time to do such work on the relatively heavy Jaguars*

Neat and tidy—the rear end view of the series three Jaguar XJ12 5.3 showing its distinctive revised rear lighting, under panels and badges

Stately and impressive low-down camera shot of the XJ12 5.3 series three, showing, among other details, its new headlight wipers

three-speed epicyclic gearbox, which gave a much more sporting response to throttle openings and almost undetectable up-changes when left to its own devices although slightly harsher down-changes from 3rd to 2nd: a much more suitable gearbox than the old Model 12s; Rolls-Royce used a similar unit.

These were the cars voted the best in the world by *CAR* magazine in 1977. They are still at the time of writing recognized as such by many enthusiasts, although their future is in doubt. Increasingly strict American fuel consumption regulations have cast a shadow over V12 production, which has always suffered whenever

there has been an energy crisis. Jaguar always thought that the V12 would run alongside the straight six in equal numbers until the first panic reaction in 1974, when production had to be cut back to only 20 per cent of the six-cylinder model. Now they might have to fit a new, more powerful, six, perhaps even a four overhead camshaft V6 version of the V12. But Jaguar and Daimler enthusiasts will always consider the V12 saloons the greatest ever. In the words of Patrick Bedard in *Car and Driver*: 'It's a car to go out and sit in when you've had a fight with your wife.' Perhaps that is all we will be able to afford to do with such a magnificent beast in years to come. . . .

Profile shot of the Daimler Double-Six showing the revised series three roofline to good effect

107

Chapter 4
'S' For Sport or Style?

The E type Jaguar became a symbol of the Swinging Sixties. It had everything: a marvellous appearance, almost unmatched performance and it was affordable. But it could not go on forever, and towards the end of that era Sir William Lyons and Malcolm Sayer—who had been responsible for some wonderful cars, including the E type—started work on its replacement. Naturally, American safety regulations had a major in-

fluence on their thinking. It was envisaged that they would sell 75 per cent of the new cars there.

When the new car was still on the drawing board during 1968 and 1969, it seemed certain that open cars would be outlawed as being unable to pass proposed roll-over tests. In 1974, such legislation against open cars was held to be an infringement on personal liberty. But the design of the XJ-S, as the new car was to be called, had already been frozen, in company with many others. That is why there is such a dearth of open cars on the market today. Although new ones are in the pipeline, demand still remains unsatisfied.

Following the decision to replace the E type with a fixed head coupé alone, other influences were brought to bear. The heating and ventilation had to be improved to saloon car standards, if not bettered, as this relatively low-volume car would certainly be expensive. Two small rear seats had

Rare view of a Malcolm Sayer design study model preceding the XJ13

A prototype XJ-S receives a severe testing at MIRA

been deemed an essential element in marketing such coupés. Stringent crash testing by the Americans dictated that it would need a crushable front and rear structure like the XJ saloons and the fuel tank would have to be mounted well out of the way of the back bumper.

It was both stylistically efficient and cost-effective to use as many XJ saloon car components as possible, or the new sporting Jaguar would be impossibly expensive. In any case, Jaguar had always followed this policy with their sports cars, with great success. The prewar sporting Jaguars and 'pre Jaguars' had a lot of components in common with the company's

The XJ-S prepares to make its debut in London

contemporary saloons; the immediate postwar trendsetter, the XK, was effectively a short-chassis Jaguar saloon; the E type that followed it shared some similar running gear to the contemporary Jaguar saloons and now the XJ-S would be rather like an XK, a short-chassis XJ. Because the new car would have to be expensive (the E type was really rather cheap because development costs had been ammortized over no

less than fourteen years!) it was decided to make it the Jaguar standard-bearer. Therefore, it was given an elaborate specification with full air conditioning as standard. This solved the twin problems of heating and ventilation.

The original XJ chassis platform was used as its basis with the wheelbase shortened to 102 inches (2590 mm), by moving the rear suspension forward under a smaller back seat pan. The front

One of the first production XJ-Ss all ready to leave Brown's Lane as XJ saloons take to their transporter

113

The XJ-S at its announcement showing clearly the impressively streamlined frontal aspect

bulkhead and engine compartment sides were modified as were the screen pillars to make the structure stronger. The engine bay was further reinforced by horizontal and diagonal tubing.

The front and rear ends of the new chassis pan were dominated by massive 5 mph (8 km/h) impact-absorbing bumpers, mounted on Menasco struts. They worked on the same principle as a conventional suspension's shock absorbers, using wax as the hydraulic medium. After severe impact, the bumpers returned to their original position more slowly than in a conventional suspension system—nevertheless the car usually straightens itself out within about half an hour! It was the first time these struts had been used on a

Engine installation of the XJ-S. No room for a battery under the bonnet!

European car.

One of the reasons the E type could not be sold in all world markets beyond 1975 was that its fuel tank was mounted in a relatively exposed position in the tail and could not have satisfied impending crash tests. Great care was taken, therefore, to ensure there would be no such problem in the forseeable future with the XJ-S. There was not enough room in its slim rear wings to use the normal XJ system, so the XJ-S's twenty-gallon tank was mounted across the rear suspension arch, well away from any impact area. The spare wheel, in its plastic cover, was mounted upright across the car, in 'front' of the tank when viewed from the luggage boot. The battery also lived in the boot, which—with typical Jaguar attention to detail—was fitted with flexible louvres in the floor. The intention was to rid the boot of stale air or even unpleasant smells if it remained closed for a long time!

Meticulous care was taken to ensure that the new car was at least as quiet as its parent saloons. The engine bay was designed to deflect noise away from the passenger compartment and even the fuel piping was masked to reduce pump noise, besides the adoption of XJ saloon-style bulkhead

Rear three-quarter view of the XJ-S emphasizing its long, low, lines

116

connections and sound-deadening material.

The suspension followed XJ saloon practice although spring rates were reduced as the short chassis car weighed around 225 lb (100 kg) less than an XJ12 at 3892 lb (1765 kg). Suspension geometry was adjusted to suit the shorter wheelbase and a 0.562-inch (14.2 mm) anti-roll bar used at the back.

The engine and transmission were the same as those in the XJ12, but Jaguar's four-speed manual gearbox was offered as an option, without over-

The interior of the XJ-S is in the best Jaguar tradition despite the dictates of modern fashion and the safety rulings of the American market

The necessarily-restricted rear seating of the XJ-S

drive. In both automatic and manual applications, a 3.07:1 limited slip differential was fitted for most markets.

The XJ12's optional alloy wheels (although painted differently) were standardized on the XJ-S with new steel-braced tyres developed by Dunlop for an even higher speed rating as their treads ran cooler than those on the normal tyres.

The XJ-Ss sold in California had to carry more comprehensive emission controls that those fitted elsewhere, which reduced power to 244 bhp (DIN) from 285 with only 269 lb/ft of torque at 4500 rpm against 294 at 3500. To make up for this potential loss in acceleration, a 3.31 rear axle ratio was fitted, with some anti-pollution devices already

Side view of a Federal version of the XJ-S showing its reinforced bumper and extra lighting

increasing fuel consumption; this brought it to around 11 mpg.

The XJ-S's braking system was the same as that on the XJ12, except that the handbrake lever was on the floor next to the driver's seat rather than working with an umbrella-style handle under the dashboard—less efficient, but more convenient to operate. The XJ-S handbrake also 'parked' flat on the floor.

The most controversial feature of the XJ-S was its appearance. Despite the care taken in the design of the XJ-S interior, it certainly did not receive universal approval. There was no wood! This should have come as no surprise to Jaguar enthusiasts. Their sports cars rarely had wooden

119

dashboards, perhaps because they don't weather well. Only the saloons, with their weather-proof interiors, have wood by tradition. But many people thought of the XJ-S as more of a slinky saloon than a sports car and expected an opulent interior like that of the larger car. The wood in a Jaguar saloon so perfectly complemented the

Connelly hide seats that the XJ-S's black vinyl padding looked cheap by comparison, and the plastic instrument panel heightened the impression. But to compensate, the seats still had leather facings and were to a new design which gave better than the saloon lateral support.

The actual instrumentation was even more

The XJ-S on the production line at Brown's Lane: still being made in the time-honoured Jaguar manner

The use of the registration number ST1 on Simon Templar's XJ-S in The Saint *television series was a particularly happy one from the point of view of publicity for Southern Television!*

comprehensive with eighteen warning lights monitoring a variety of functions, with red for 'emergency imminent' and amber for 'check when convenient'.

Although less controversial than the interior, the outward appearance of the new car also attracted criticism. It was the first Jaguar that did not automatically receive rave reviews in the American motoring press. Perhaps that was because it bore a resemblance to a Chevrolet Camaro (a good-looking car in its own right) rather than being obviously European like a Ferrari. The shape, however was very efficient, with an even lower drag factor than the aircraft-

Last of a line? The XJ-S as it entered the 1980s

inspired E type. And it must be remembered that there are now so many design restrictions (such as bumper heights) that weary designers are saying all they have to do now is to take some headlights and a bumper and hang a car on the back.

As it happened, the headlights fitted to all except XJ-Ss destined for America were very good. Especially designed for the beautifully streamlined nose by the French firm Cibie, with twin halogen bulbs (one for dip and one for main beam), they gave a magnificent spread of light. Incredibly short-sighted American legislation forbade their use in the land of the free and necessitated the fitting of an ordinary four-headlight system of much inferior performance.

This was the car that won the 1979 Cannonball coast-to-coast dash in which chosen teams hammered a variety of vehicles from New York to California in the shortest possible time, regardless of Smokey and the law en route, and of which Patrick Bedard (again!) said in *Car and Driver*: 'It's extravagant—a car that will cruise happily at 140 mph (when the speed limit is 55); all the more reason to want one.'

It is also the car on which Jaguar might well base their sporting future as Pinifarina has already produced a remodelled XJ-S with an open top. The Italian styling firm's Jaguar XJ-S Spider, shown at the 1978 Birmingham Motor Show, is precisely the sort of car that Jaguar might consider building. The XJ-S was partly the result of the predicament which faced them after the death of Malcolm Sayer in 1969 and Sir William Lyons's retirement in 1972. Sir William committed the company to the XJ-S shape but for production it was finalized by a committee in 1975. It exemplifies how committee decisions so often fall between stools: hence the controversial appearance of the XJ-S today. Pininfarina pro-

duced the XJ-S Spider independently, as if to persuade British Leyland that it was time to produce the open Jaguar which so many enthusiasts are crying out for. The actual chassis for the Spider is that of a well-used, ex-works development hack. After removing the original panels, Pininfarina made relatively few changes to the floor pan and internal structure. The biggest change is the position of the fuel tank, below the luggage boot floor, to enable the Spider to be a truly open car. The sills are strengthened, but Pininfarina claims that the car could be made lighter than a standard XJ-S with a consequent improvement in performance, ability to withstand crash testing, and (even more important) fuel consumption. Alternatively a lighter XJ-S could well use a V6 version of the existing V12!

Whatever happens, it seems as though there is a lot of life left in the XJ range yet.

Success at last for the V12 in competition: the Group 44 XJ-S of Bob Tullius pictured winning at Mosport in 1977 on the way to a TransAm championship

Specifications

Jaguar XJ6 2.8-litre De Luxe

Engine: front, 4 stroke; cylinders: 6, vertical, in line; bore and stroke: 83.1 × 86.1 mm, 3.27 × 3.39 in; engine capacity: 2790.71 cc, 170.30 cu in; compression ratio: 9 to 1; max. power (SAE): 180 bhp at 6000 rpm; max. torque (SAE): 182 lb/ft, 25.1 kg/m at 3750 rpm; max. engine rpm: 6800; specific power: 64.5 hp/1; cylinder block: cast iron, dry liners; cylinder head: light alloy, hemispherical combustion chambers; crankshaft bearings: 7; valves: 2 per cylinder, overhead, vee-slanted at 70 degrees, thimble tappets; camshafts: 2, overhead; lubrication: mechanical pump, full-flow filter; lubrication system capacity: 14.50 Imp pt, 8.2 litres, 17.33 US pt; carburation: 2 SU type HD8 horizontal carburettors; fuel feed: electric pump; cooling system: water, thermostatic fan; cooling system capacity: 30 Imp pt, 17 litres, 35.94 US pt.

Transmission: clutch: single dry plate (diaphragm), hydraulically controlled; gearbox: mechanical; gears: 4 plus reverse; synchromesh on all forward gears; gearbox ratios: first 2.933, second 1.905, third 1.389, fourth 1, reverse 3.378; gear lever, central; final drive; hypoid bevel; axle ratio, 4.270.

Chassis: integral, front and rear sub-frames; front suspension: independent, wishbones, lower trailing links, coil springs, anti-roll bar, telescopic dampers, rear suspension, independent, wishbones, semi-axle as upper arm, trailing lower radius arms, 4 coil springs, 4 telescopic dampers. Steering rack and pinion, adjustable steering wheel, variable ratio servo; turns of steering wheel, lock to lock: 3.50; turning circle, left 37 ft 5 in, 1140 mm; right 36 ft 8in, 1120 mm

Brakes: disc (front diameter 11.80 in, 300 mm, rear 10.40 in, 264 mm); dual circuit, servo; area rubbed by linings: front 242.40 sq in, 1563.48 sq cm, rear 193.20 sq in, 1246.14 sq cm, total 435.60 sq in, 2809.62 sq cm.

Electrical equipment: voltage: 12; battery: 51 Ah; generator type: alternator, 45 Ah; ignition distributor: Lucas; headlamps: 4.

Dimensions and weight: wheelbase: 108.87 in, 2765 mm; front track: 58 in, 1473 mm; rear track: 58.33 in, 1482 mm; overall length: 189.60 in, 4816 mm; overall width: 69.75 in, 1772 mm; overall height: 52.87 in, 1343 mm; ground clearance: 6 in, 152 mm; dry weight 3389 lb, 1537 kg; width of rims: 6 in, 152 mm; tyres 750 × 15; fuel tank capacity: 23 Imp gal, 105 litres, 27.7 US gal.

Body: saloon/sedan; doors: 4; seats: 5; front seats: separate, reclining backrests.

Performance: (factory figures) max speeds; 41 mph (66 km/h) in first gear; 63.5 mph (102.2 km/h) in second gear; 87 mph (140 km/h) in third gear; 118 mph (190 km/h) in fourth gear; power-weight ratio: 18.7 lb/hp, 8.5 kg/hp; carrying capacity: 882 lb, 400 kg, acceleration: standing quarter mile 17.7 sec, 0–50 mph (0–80 km/h) 8.5 sec; speed in direct drive at 1000 rpm: 17.8 mph (28.7 km/h).

Running: fuel; 98–100 oct petrol; engine sump oil: 13.50 Imp pt, 7.7 litre, 16.28 US pt. SAE 10W-40 (winter), 20W-50 (summer), change every 3000 miles, 4800 km; gearbox oil: 2.50 Imp pt, 1.4 litres, 2.96 US pt, SAE 30, change every 10,000 miles, 16,100 km; final drive oil: 2.75 Imp pt, 1.6 litres, 3.38 US pt, SAE 90, change every 10,000 miles, 16,100 km; tappet clearances: inlet 0.004 in, 0.10 mm, exhaust 0.006 in, 0.15 mm; valve timing: inlet opens 15 degrees before top dead centre and closes 57 degrees after bottom dead centre, exhaust opens 57 degrees before bottom dead centre and closes 15 degrees after top dead centre.

Variations and optional accessories: 8:1 compression ratio; Laycock-de Normanville overdrive on fourth gear (0.779) ratio), 4.550 axle ratio; Borg Warner 35 automatic gearbox, hydraulic torque converter and planetary gears with three ratios (first 2.389, second 1.450, third 1, reverse 2.089) max. ratio of converter at stall 2, possible manual selection, max. speeds (first) 51 mph (82.1 km/h), second 83 mph (134.4 km/h), third 118 mph (190 km/h).

Price in Great Britain on introduction in Otober 1968: £1483 basic, £1938 with tax; in 1969 £1608, £2090; in 1970 £1823, £2370; in 1971 £2058, £2676; in 1972 and 1973 £2285, £2960.

Jaguar XJ6 2.8 litre standard

As Jaguar XJ6 De Luxe except more spartan interior; optional extras, 8:1 compression ratio; power-assisted steering; reclining backrests; Laycock de Normanville overdrive in fourth gear; and Borg Warner Model 35 automatic gearbox.

Price in Great Britain on introduction in October 1968 (basic, with tax): £1405, £1797; in 1969 £1530, £1989; in 1970 £1745, £2268; in 1971 £1963, £2552.

Jaguar XJ6 4.2-litre

As XJ6 2.8-litre De Luxe except:

Engine: bore and stroke: 92.1 × 106 mm, 3.63 × 4.17 in; engine capacity: 4235 cc, 258.42 cu in; compression ratio: 8 to 1; max. power (SAE) 245 bhp at 5400 rpm; max torque (SAE) 283 lb/ft, 39.1 kg/m at 4000 rpm; max. engine rpm, 6000; specific power: 62.6 hp/1, cooling system capacity: 25.40 Imp pt, 14.4 litres, 30.44 US pt. 7 or 9:1 compression ratio optional.

Transmission: 3.540 axle ratio, optional Borg Warner Model 8 automatic gearbox, hydraulic torque converter and planetary gears with three ratios (first 2.401, second 1.458, third 1, reverse 2), max ratio of converter at stall 2, possible manual selection.

Electrical equipment: 60 Ah battery.

Dimension and weight: 3444 lb, 1562 kg.

Performance (factory figures): max speeds, first 44 mph (70.8 km/h), second 67 mph, (107.9 km/h), third 92 mph (148.1 km/h), fourth 127 mph (204.5 km/h); power-weight ratio 13.2 lb/hp, 6 kg/hp; acceleration standing start quarter mile 16.3 sec, 0–50 mph (0–80 km/h) 6.5 sec, speed in direct drive at 1000 rpm 21.4 mph (34.4 km/h); with automatic transmission, max speeds, first 53.5 mph (86.1 km/h), second 88 mph (141.7 km/h), third 127 mph (204.5 km/h).

Price in Great Britain on introduction in September 1968 (basic with tax): £1762, £2253; in 1969 £1894, £2447; in 1970 £2059, £2672 (United States $6585); in 1971 £2288, £2974 (United States $7683); in 1972 £2540, £3302 (United States $8716).

From early 1970, options included air conditioning and the Borg Warner model 12 automatic gearbox in place of the Model 8, and a 3.31 rear axle ratio. Performance figures with the Model 12 gearbox: max speeds, first 53 mph (85 km/h), second 88 mph (142 km/h), third 121 mph (195 km/h). Long wheelbase option from October 1972.

**Daimler Sovereign
2.8-litre**

As Jaguar XJ6 2.8-litre De Luxe except:
Price on introduction in October 1969 (basic, with tax):
£1803, £2344; in 1970 £1958, £2545; in 1971 £2202, £2862;
in 1972 £2443, £3176; Air conditioning optional.

**Daimler Sovereign
4.2-litre**

As Jaguar XJ6 4.2-litre except:
Price on introduction in October 1969 (basic, with tax):
£2046, £2660; in 1970 £2194, £2852; in 1971 £2430, 3154; in
1972 £2696, £3505. Long wheelbase option from October
1972.

Jaguar XJ12

As Jaguar XJ6 4.2-litre except:
Engine: 12 cylinders, Vee-slanted at 60 degrees; 5343 cc,
326 cu in, (90 × 70 mm, 3.54 × 2.76 in); compression ratio: 9
to 1; max. power (DIN): 272 bhp at 5850 rpm; max torque
(DIN) 304 lb/ft, 41.9 kg/m at 3600 rpm; max. engine rpm:
6500; specific power 50.9 hp/l; cylinder block: light alloy
with wet liners; cylinder head: light alloy with
hemispherical combustion chambers; crankshaft
bearings: 7; valves: in line thimble tappets; camshafts: 1
per cylinder block, overhead; lubrication: gear pump, full
flow filter, 17.6 Imp pt, 10 litres, 21.1 US pt; 4 Zenith 175
CDSE variable choke side-draught carburettors; fuel feed:
electric pump; Cooling system capacity: 36 Imp pt, 20.5
litres, 43.3 US pt.
Transmission: automatic only.
Performance (factory figures) max speeds: first 65 mph,
104 km/h; second 102 mph, 164 km/h; third 140 mph,
225 km/h; power-weight ratio: 6.4 lb/hp, 2.9 kg/hp;
acceleration standing quarter mile, 15.7 sec, 0–50 mph
(0–80 km/h) 6.1 sec; speed in direct drive at 1000 rpm
22.9 mph, 36.9 km/h.
Dimensions and weight: 1760 lb, 798 kg.
Running: engine sump oil: 16 Imp pt, 9.1 litres, 19.2 US
pt; gearbox oil: 2.8 Imp pt, 1.6 litres, 3.4 US pt, no change
recommended; final drive oil: 2.6 Imp pt, 1.5 litres, 3.2 US
pt, SAE 90.
Price on introduction in Great Britain in July 1972:
£3082, £4007.

Daimler Double Six

As Jaguar XJ12 except:
Price: £3184, £4139 (basic, with tax).

**Daimler Double Six
Vanden Plas**

As Daimler Double Six, except:
Price: £4500, £5850 (basic, with tax).

129

Jaguar XJ6 4.2-litre series II

As Jaguar XJ6 4.2-litre except:
Dimensions and weight: wheelbase: 108.80 in, 2760 mm (as long wheelbase option on earlier cars); length 190.70 in, 4840 mm; weight 3914 lb, 1775 kg.
Performance: (factory figures) max speeds; first 40 mph, 64 km/h; second 62 mph, 99 km/h; third 85 mph, 136 km/h; fourth 117 mph, 189 km/h; overdrive 130 mph, 210 km/h; power-weight ratio: 21.6 lb/ft, 9.8 kg/hp; speed in direct drive at 1000 rpm, 21.4 mph, 34.4 kph. Fuel injection from May 1978.
Price on introduction in Great Britain in September 1973 (basic, with tax): £3674, £4776; in 1974 £4645, £6039, in United States $11,500; in 1975 £5615, £7300; in United States $13,000; in 1976 £7125, £9263, in United States $15,000; in 1977 £8651, £11,246, United States $16,500; in 1978 £10,209, £13,272, United States $20,000.

Daimler Sovereign 4.2-litre series II

As Jaguar XJ6 4.2-litre series II except:
Price on introduction in Great Britain in September 1973 (basic, with tax): £3784, £4919; in 1974 £4767, £1430; in 1975 £5823, £7570; in 1976 £7397, £9617; in 1977 £9065, £11,785; in 1978 £10,733, £13,953.

Jaguar XJ12 series II

As Jaguar XJ6 series II, except engine and performance as Jaguar XJ12, and **price** on introduction in Great Britain in September 1973 (basic, with tax): £4702, £6113; in 1974 £5491, £7138, in United States $13,500; in 1975 £7046, £9186; in 1976 £8788, £11,424, in United States $17,250; in 1977 £10,668, £13,868, in United States $17,750; in 1978 £12,436, £16,167, in United States $22,000.

Daimler Double Six series II

As Jaguar XJ12 series II, except **price** on introduction in Great Britain in September 1973 (basic, with tax): £4812, £6256; in 1974 £5612, £7296; in 1975 £7197, £9356; in 1976 £9059, £11,777; in 1977 £11,102, £14,443; in 1978 £12,991, £16,888.

Jaguar XJ6C

As Jaguar XJ6 series II except two-door bodywork, **wheelbase** 108.87 in, 2760 mm; length 190.70 in, 4840 mm; **dry weight** 3861 lb, 1751 kg; **power weight ratio** 21.4 lb/hp, 9.7 kg/hp.
Price on introduction in Great Britain in April 1975 (basic, with tax): £6009, £7811; in 1976 £7625, £9913.

Jaguar XJ12C

As Jaguar XJ6C except **dry weight** 4046 lb, 1835 kg; **power-weight ratio** 16.1 lb/hp, 7.3 kg/hp. **Price** on introduction in Great Britain in 1974 (basic, with tax): £6009, £7811; in 1975 £7572, £9844; in 1976 £9417, £12,242.

Daimler Sovereign series II 4.2C

As Jaguar XJ6C except: **Price** on introduction in Great Britain in 1974 (basic, with tax): £4899, £6369; in 1975 £6195, £8054; in 1976 £7895, £10,264.

Daimler Double Six 5.3C

As Jaguar XJ12C except: **Price** on introduction in Great Britain in 1975 (basic, with tax): £7693, £10,001; in 1976 £9688, £12,594.

Daimler Double Six series II Vanden Plas 5.3-litre saloon

As Daimler Double Six series II except: **dry weight** 4116 lb, 1821 kg; **power-weight ratio** 16.1 lb/hp, 7.3 kg/hp. **Price** on introduction in Great Britain in 1973 (basic, with tax): £6068, £6688; in 1974 £7334, £9534; in 1975 £9117, £11,852; in 1976 £11,068, £14,388; in 1977 £14,583, £18,958; in 1978 £16,791, £21,828.

Daimler Sovereign 4.2-litre Vanden Plas

As Jaguar XJ6C except **price** on introduction in 1976 (basic, with tax): £9887, £12,653.

Jaguar XJ6 3.4-litre saloon

As Jaguar XJ6 series II saloon except: **Engine:** front, four-stroke; 6 cylinders, vertical, in-line; 3442 cc, 210 cu. in (83 × 106 mm, 3.28 × 4.17 in); compression ratio 8.8:1; max. power (DIN) 161 bhp at 5000 rpm; max. torque (DIN) 189 lb/ft, 26.1 kg/m at 3500 rpm; max. engine rpm 5500; 46.8 hp/litre; cast iron dry liners, light alloy head, hemispherical combustion chambers; seven crankshaft bearings; valves: overhead, Vee-slanted, thimble tappets; camshafts, two, overhead; lubrication: rotary pump, full-flow filter, oil cooler, 14.5 Imp pt, 8.2 litres, 17.3 US pt; two SU type HS8 horizontal carburettors; fuel feed two electric pumps; water-cooled, 32.5 Imp pt, 18.4 litres, 38.9 US pt; viscous coupling thermostatic fan. **Transmission:** gearbox, manual four ratios plus overdrive: first 3.238, second 1.905, third 1.389, fourth 1; overdrive 0.779, reverse 3.428; rear axle ratio 3.54. Optional Borg Warner Model 65 automatic gearbox, ratios: first 2.4, second 1.460, third 1, reverse 2; max ratio of converter at stall, 2; possible manual selection; optional rear axle ratios with automatic gearbox: 3.07 or 3.31.

Performance: (factory figures) max. speeds with manual gearbox: first 36 mph, 58 km/h; second 62 mph, 99 km/h; third 85 mph, 136 km/h; acceleration: standing quarter mile 18 sec, 0–50 mph (0–80 km/h) 8.7 sec; with automatic gearbox: standing quarter mile 18.6 sec; max. speed 115 mph, 184 km/h; speed in direct drive at 1000 rpm, 21.4 mph, 34.4 km/h.

Dimensions as Jaguar XJ6 series II, weight: 3715 lb, 1685 kg.

Price on introduction in Great Britain in April 1975 (basic, with tax): £5198, £6757 with tax; in 1976 £6622, £8609; in 1977 £8174, £10,626; in 1978 £9662, £12,559.

Jaguar XJ-S

Engine and transmission as Jaguar XJ12.

Performance (factory figures): max. speeds, first 50 mph, 80 km/h; second 80 mph, 128 km/h; third 103 mph, 165 km/h; fourth 150 mph, 241 km/h; power-weight ratio; 13 lb/hp, 5.9 kg/hp; acceleration: standing quarter mile, 14.5 sec, 0–60 mph (0–80 km/h) 4.8 sec; speed in direct drive at 1000 rpm 24.8 mph, 39.9 km/h.

Chassis: integral, front and rear subframes, front suspension: independent, wishbones, lower trailing links, coil springs, anti-roll bar, telescopic dampers; rear: independent, lower wishbones, semi-axles as upper arms, trailing lower radius arms, four coil springs, four telescopic dampers, anti-roll bar.

Brakes as Jaguar XJ12.

Dimensions and weight: wheelbase, 102 in, 2590 mm; front track 58 in, 1470 mm; rear 58.60 in, 1490 mm; length 191.70 in, 4870 mm; width 70.60 in, 1790 mm; height 49.65 in, 1260 mm; ground clearance 5.50 in, 140 mm; weight 3710 lb, 1682 kg; turning circle 36 ft, 11 metres.

Price on introduction in Great Britain in April 1975 (basic, with tax): £8900, £11,660, in United States $19,000; in 1976 £11,243, £14,616, in United States $20,250; in 1977 £13,200, £17,160, in United States $21,700; in 1978 £15,149, £19,694, in United States $25,000.

Production

Series I			First/last known chassis no.	Approx. total
Jaguar	swb	2.8	IG 1001/14301	13,300
	swb	4.2	IL 1001/34467	33,466
	swb	5.3	IP 1001/1720	719
Daimler	swb	2.8	IT 1001/4069	3068
	swb	4.2	IU 1001/11894	10,893
Jaguar	lwb	4.2	2E 1001/1583	582
	lwb	5.3	2C 1001/1750	749
Daimler	lwb	4.2	2D 1001/1394	393
	lwb	5.3	2A 1001/1524	523
Vanden Plas		5.3	2B 1001/1337	336

Series II				
Jaguar	swb	4.2	2N 1001/8463	7462
Daimler	swb	4.2	2M 1001/3313	2312
Jaguar	lwb	4.2	2T 1001/?	?
	lwb	3.4	3A 1001/?	?
	lwb	5.3	2R 1001/?	?
Daimler	lwb	4.2	2S 1001/?	?
	lwb	3.4	3B 1001/3344	2343
Vanden Plas		4.2	3C 1001/?	?
		5.3	2P 1001/?	?
Jaguar	C	4.2	2J 1001/3606	2605
	C	5.3	2G 1001/1604	603
Daimler	C	4.2	2H 1001/2586	1585
	C	5.3	2F 1001/1372	371

Note: No figures are available as such. Production totals have been arrived at by subtracting the first from the last chassis numbers. This is full of pitfalls because there were often gaps of unallocated chassis numbers and some early cars of each model were used for development and crash testing. Also just prior to the end of Series II production a new VIN system (Vehicle Identification Number) was implemented to comply with new EEC legislation. This system does not separate different models.

Acknowledgements

Rather special circumstances in the publishing of this book required all those people listed below to work harder and faster in supplying photographs than any editor could normally expect. Many of them also supplied information to the author at a more leisurely pace. It cannot be repeated enough—a sincere thank you.

Paul Skilleter, Editor of the *Jaguar Driver* Magazine. Andrew Whyte formerly PR Manager of Jaguar Cars Limited; Alan Hodge and his staff currently conducting 'Special Facilities' at Jaguar Cars; Frenchman Jean-François Marchet; photographers Andrew Bell, Neill Bruce and Nicky Wright; the National Motor Museum, Carrozzeria Bertone, Carrozzeria Pininfarina, Michael Frostick and Mike Cook of the American end of Jaguar Cars. Finally, Rick Reading, a Director of the Jaguar Drivers' Club and Secretary of the XJ Register, provided invaluable help.

Index